Birds of
Trinidad and Tobago

Richard ffrench

CARIBBEAN

© Copyright text and illustrations Richard ffrench, 1986

All rights reserved. No reproduction copy or transmission of
this publication may be made without written permission.

No paragraph of this publication may be reproduced, copied or
transmitted save with written permission or in accordance with
the provisions of the Copyright, Designs and Patents Act 1988,
or under the terms of any licence permitting limited copying issued
by the Copyright Licensing Agency, 90 Tottenham Court Road,
London W1P 9HE.

Any persons who does any unauthorised act in relation to this
publication may be liable to criminal prosecution and civil claims
for damages.

First published 1986
Reprinted 1988, 1990, 1991, 1992, 1993, 1994 (twice)

Published by MACMILLAN EDUCATION LTD
London and Basingstoke
*Associated companies and representatives in Accra , Auckland, Cairo,
Delhi, Dublin, Freetown, Gaborone, Hamburg, Harare, Hong Kong,
Kampala, Lagos, Lahore, Lusaka, Manzini, Melbourne, Mexico City,
Nairobi, New York, São Paulo, Singapore, Tokyo*

ISBN 0–333–40912–4

Printed in Malaysia.

A catalogue record for this book is available from
the British Library.

Contents

TOBAGO

ST. GILES IS.

CHARLOTTEVILLE X

0 ——— 5 Miles

ROXBOROUGH-BLOODY
BAY RD
X

LITTLE
TOBAGO

HILLSBOROUGH
DAM
X

X PLYMOUTH

X GRAFTON
X MT IRVINE   SCARBOROUGH
X BUCCOO   X
STORE   SMITH'S IS.
BAY X X BON ACCORD
       FRIENDSHIP
            X

TRINIDAD

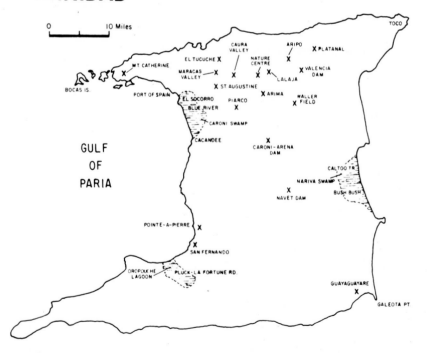

0 ——— 10 Miles

TOCO

CAURA
VALLEY   ARIPO
                X   X PLATANAL
MT CATHERINE   EL TUCUCHE X
   X   NATURE   X VALENCIA
MARACAS   CENTRE   DAM
VALLEY X   X   X LALAJA
BOCAS IS.   X ST AUGUSTINE
PORT OF SPAIN   X ARIMA   WALLER
         EL SOCORRO   FIELD
         BLUE RIVER   PIARCO   X
              X CARONI SWAMP X
         CACANDEE

GULF   X
                  CARONI-ARENA
 OF   DAM
                                    CALTOO TR
PARIA   NARIVA SWAMP
                                    BUSH BUSH
                        X
                     NAVET DAM

         POINTE-A-PIERRE X

              X
         SAN FERNANDO
OROPOUCHE   X PLUCK-LA FORTUNE RD.
LAGOON   GUAYAGUAYARE
                                      X
                              GALEOTA PT

Preface

This book treats 83 species of birds, mostly the more common ones, from Trinidad and Tobago; 35 of these are also found in the eastern Caribbean. There is a brief introduction which covers the basic facts about local birds: the numbers of families and species that may be found in Trinidad and Tobago; their relationships to birds of the mainland and other islands; migration; habitats; ecology. The parts of a bird are described and habits, such as flocking, feeding, roosting, nesting, display, rivalry, parasitism and predation are discussed. Information is given about how to watch birds, the equipment needed, photography and conservation. Advice on where to go in Trinidad and Tobago to see birds is included (with maps). Finally, a short bibliography is given at the end of the Introduction.

The text divides the birds into seven groups according to their habitats: gardens and parks; open country and scrubland; cultivated land with large trees; the forest; swamps, marshes and reservoirs; the coast; the air (comprising those species most commonly seen soaring or feeding in the sky).

Each species is treated similarly. Both the English and the scientific names are given, and some local names are included. The length and a simple field description is given for each bird. Where appropriate, details of voice, habitat and range, and migratory habits are noted. Details of diet, habits, roosting and/or nesting are also given, along with any unusual aspects of behaviour.

Each species is illustrated by a colour photograph; the great majority of these were taken on location in Trinidad or Tobago. Where the male and female of a species differ in appearance, the sex of the bird in the photograph is given in the caption.

Acknowledgements

The author and publishers wish to thank the following for the use of their photographs:
G. Powell;
K. Michell;
R.G. Gibbs;
W. Davidson;
B. Hannah;
D.J. Montier.
E. Hosking
M.D. England
J. ffrench

Introduction

Among the islands of the West Indies, Trinidad and Tobago provide a fascinating opportunity for anyone interested in natural history, particularly birds. Trinidad's position — a mere ten miles distant from the South American mainland — means that its flora and fauna are essentially continental in nature. The great variety of species that is typical of the South American region is also present in Trinidad and, to a lesser degree, in nearby Tobago.

In addition, the position of the islands, at the southern end of the Antillean island chain, means that many northern migratory birds stay or pass through on their way to wintering grounds in the south. Furthermore, several southern species migrate north from Argentina to Venezuela or the Guianas during the austral winter, and some of these regularly visit Trinidad and Tobago.

Although both islands are small, they contain a wide variety of habitats, including tropical rain forest, swamp forest, semi-deciduous forest, mangrove swamp, freshwater marshland and savannah. Some of these habitats are not very extensive, but each is large enough to support a distinct population of birds.

As a result of these factors, the number of bird families and species which are found on the two islands is quite large in relation to their size. Over 400 species from 65 families have been recorded in Trinidad, while over 180 species are known in Tobago. Over 250 species breed in Trinidad, and about 90 in Tobago. Altogether, more than 420 species are listed for both islands, some 20 of which are known only on Tobago.

About the same number of species is recorded for the rest of the West Indies — including the Bahamas. Many of the Antillean islands have comparatively few species but, because of their small size, their isolation and their restricted habitat, these tend to include a high proportion of endemic species. By contrast, Trinidad has only one (doubtful) endemic species, and Tobago has none.

As mentioned earlier, migrants form a significant proportion of the birds of Trinidad and Tobago. The great majority — about 100 species — come from their breeding grounds in the north. Most arrive between August and October, some passing through after a brief or perhaps extended rest, the others staying during the northern winter months.

In about April they return north, many species travelling further to the west on the return journey.

Fewer species — about 40 in all — visit from the south, but some of these breed in nearby Venezuela, so their migration to our islands is just a temporary dispersal of population. These southern visitors may arrive as early as January and most of them have left by September.

Ecology

It is important for the student of birds to recognise the relationship between the habitat of a species and its life history. Clearly, a bird will live in a place in which it can find the food that suits it, and it will nest where suitable material and a site can be found. Thus, in the study of birds one needs to learn more than the mere details of plumage and voice; attention should also be paid to the precise details of where the bird feeds and what it feeds on.

With knowledge of these details, one can eventually build up a thorough understanding of a bird's environment and needs. This can even assist in identification, since a particular species is highly unlikely to be found in an unsuitable habitat. A positive identification may be made by realising that only one of the species fitting a description is likely to be found in that habitat.

Describing birds

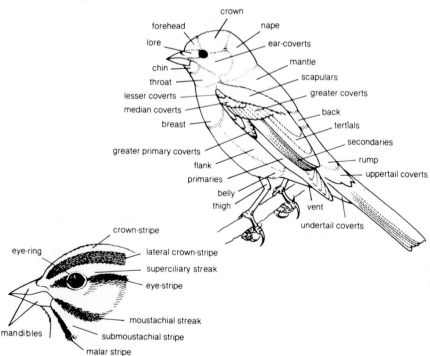

It is helpful to know the correct terms which are used to describe the parts of a bird (see page 2). In this book, the average length of an adult (from beak to tail) is given in both inches and centimetres. Where appropriate, the wingspan (from wing-tip to wing-tip) of a flying bird is included.

The habits of birds

The habits of birds are particularly interesting and can usually be observed quite easily. A few of the most noticeable habits are described below.

Some species like to congregate in flocks when feeding, flying or roosting. These flocks may be very large, as in the case of roosting grackles, or quite small, as in a family party of anis. Flocking can be an advantage to a species as a defence against an enemy or as a means of communicating information about food. However, flocking is by no means universal; some birds never form a group larger than an individual family.

Understanding a bird's diet involves the knowledge of how it obtains its food, which can be a fascinating area of study in itself. For example, an insect-eater may catch flying insects in mid-air, pick them up from the ground, find them inside tree-holes or under bark, search for them on the undersides of leaves, or dig down into soil or mud to extract them. As a group, birds feed on flesh, fish, molluscs, worms, reptiles, invertebrates, eggs, fruit, leaves, seeds and nectar — and on each other. However, individual species are often very specific in their diet, so a captive bird which is given unsuitable food may die without touching it.

Little is known about the sleeping habits of many birds; they seem to just disappear when darkness approaches. Many people mistakenly assume that at night birds return to their nests; this is generally only the case for an incubating or brooding parent during the nesting period (the Bananaquit being a notable exception). It is likely that many species find shelter amidst vegetation or in a tree-hole, and sleep there. Some prefer to roost collectively, and the study of such communal roosting can be very interesting.

Breeding behaviour in birds can be quite complex and each species tends to conform to a particular pattern. There are many different ways in which birds select their partners, establish a breeding territory, choose a nest-site and build a nest, lay and incubate the eggs, and feed and care for the young. Nests themselves vary immensely in form, even within Trinidad and Tobago, to include not only the well-known cup-shaped type, but also, among others, spheres with side entrances, bags, tubes, mounds and hammocks; some birds build no

3

nest at all, or merely construct a 'token' nest at the site where they lay their eggs. The nest-sites and materials used are also extremely varied. Some young are precocial, that is, they are capable of leaving the nest and feeding themselves within a few hours of hatching. Others remain in the nest, helpless and entirely dependent on parental attention during the fledging period which may last from nine days (in small finches) to more than three months (in the Oilbird).

One of the most interesting facets of breeding behaviour concerns the manifestations of rivalry and advertisement, usually called display. The male attracts the attention of his mate, or stimulates her towards sexual activity, by displaying particularly colourful parts of his plumage or other physical attributes. Occasionally, the female may join him in a mutual display; she rarely initiates the behaviour. The song of a male bird is a type of display, and is often associated with display movements. Forms of display vary almost as much as plumage, and are sometimes so specific that they can become an aid to identification of the bird. Certain displays are aimed more at impressing rival males. Some male birds, such as manakins and hermit hummingbirds, congregate to display together. These displays are known as leks. Several examples of this behaviour occur in Trinidad and Tobago, and some have formed the subjects of very interesting studies.

The delicate balance and precision needed for efficient aerial manoeuvre require that a bird maintains its feathers in the best possible condition; therefore, birds continually preen themselves, not only for hygiene, but also to ensure the correct positioning of feathers, particularly the flight feathers. They use their oil glands to help preserve waterproofing. In addition to normal wear, the feathers may also suffer damage, so all feathers are regularly shed and renewed by the process of moulting, which, in the case of most local birds, occurs once a year. Since moulting birds are sometimes handicapped by the absence of one or more flight feathers, it is not surprising to find that the moult period usually occurs *after* a breeding season which is a time in which parent birds are required to be especially active to feed and care for their young. Birds may be more than usually quiet and subdued during their moulting period, so are less likely to be seen.

Inter-specific relations among birds also form a subject of interest. Certain species feed on others, and these predatory birds, such as hawks, falcons and owls, include some of the most spectacular and attractive birds in the country. Perhaps we are less inclined, emotionally, to appreciate the way in which certain species steal the eggs or nestlings of other birds, but it is of course all part of Nature's infinitely varied design. A most intriguing form of predation is shown in the

4

parasitic behaviour of some birds, which literally steal food from the mouths of others, or appropriate their nests (before they have completed their breeding cycle), or even, as in the case of the cowbirds and some cuckoos, deposit eggs in other birds' nests, for the hosts to incubate and nurture.

Watching birds

It may be useful to lay down certain principles for the aspiring birdwatcher to follow in order to make the best use of the available opportunities. Obviously it helps if you know the best way to approach birds; you also need to know where to go from there.

A birdwatcher must try to be inconspicuous, to avoid alarming the birds he or she is watching. Therefore, he or she must wear suitable clothing, keep as quiet as possible and move as little as possible. Many birds soon become familiar with a stationary object, so losing the inhibitions that normally cause them to fly away. When walking in the forest or in thick cover, it is especially important to be silent because forest birds are very aware of sound which is their own principal means of communication.

In the tropics, it is particularly important to look for birds either in the first half of the morning or during the last two hours of daylight. Many birds, especially those in open areas, tend to stay under cover, where it is cooler, during the hot, middle hours of the day. Probably the best time for birdwatching is between 6 a.m. and 9 a.m.

Although it is not essential to use binoculars or a telescope for birdwatching, these aids will improve your view and enable you to see and recognise much that would otherwise escape your notice. There are many types of binoculars, and a wide price range reflecting the varied quality. Beginners should avoid binoculars that are too heavy, since one needs to cultivate rapid coordination of eye and hand for the best results. The most convenient size is 8 × 30, but 7 × 35 or 8 × 40 will also do. Those with magnification of 10 × are often difficult to keep steady. A telescope is best used with a tripod over a fixed field of view, such as mud-flats, marshes or the sea. But remember that, in the tropics, heat haze often obscures low-level viewing.

Just as important a piece of equipment is the notebook. There is no substitute for making your own notes, if you want to remember details accurately. It also ensures that you record what you actually *see* — if you make it a rule to make your own notes *before* checking a guidebook for help in identification. Notes should be as full as is convenient, and, ideally, they should include details of plumage, size, call-notes, behaviour, habitat, location, time and conditions when sighted. Here it is useful to share your birdwatching experiences with a companion, since this tends to lessen the chances of errors in observation. This is particularly important where rare birds are concerned. One way of finding birdwatching companions is to join a club, such as the Trinidad and Tobago Field Naturalists' Club, where you will meet people with similar interests.

A word of warning about bird photography. Although photographs of birds can be useful and decorative, they can also be extremely difficult to obtain. It has been said that you can't be a good bird-watcher and a bird-photographer at the same time, as the two activities tend to exclude each other. Certainly photographers should be careful not to put their own interest in getting a good bird picture before the safety and welfare of their subject. This is especially important with nesting birds, which are liable to desert their nests if disturbed.

Where to watch birds in Trinidad and Tobago

Some of the many good locations for birdwatching in our islands stand out as better than most (see maps, page iv). To see swamp and marsh birds in Trinidad you should go to Caroni Swamp (access is possible by boat) or to adjoining marshes at El Socorro, Blue River and Cacandee. Nariva Swamp is also a good place to see marsh birds, but it is less accessible. The edges may be approached at Caltoo Trace and near Bush-Bush. Oropouche Lagoon is particularly rewarding in the wet season; access can be gained from the Pluck-La Fortune Road.

Trinidad's Northern Range has many access points, too numerous to mention here, along the roads and trails that go up the various valleys. Outstanding areas are the Arima Valley, including the Asa Wright Nature Centre, Lalaja Road and the Maracas and Caura Valleys which have trails leading to El Tucuche. The Aripo and Cumaca Roads lead to interesting locations on the slopes of Mount Aripo and in the Platanal. Different birds may be found in the northwest, at Mount Catherine, or on the Bocas islands. Forest birds of a different kind may also be found in the low-lying areas of Arena, Guayaguayare and the oil-fields in the south and southwest.

Reservoirs and mud-flats are always good places to see water-birds. If you are fortunate enough to be able to visit the Valencia, Navet or Caroni-Arena dams, or the Pointe-a-Pierre reservoirs, you stand a good chance of seeing some interesting birds.

Certain species thrive well in suburban habitats; you should go to Pointe-a-Pierre, St Augustine or the cities of Port of Spain or San Fernando to see these. But birds need vegetation of course, so they will be found mostly in such places as parks or golf-courses. The Queen's Park Savannah and Botanic Gardens in Port of Spain provide the right habitat for a number of species.

Savannah birds are best found on large areas of open ground, such as Waller Field and Piarco, but in the dry season you will not see many because most will have moved to nearby marshland. Many savannah birds seem to associate to some extent with cattle, so cattle ranches often contain some interesting bird life.

To see seabirds off the coast of Trinidad you will need to visit the Gulf of Paria, Toco, Nariva river mouth or Galeota Point. However, the seabird enthusiast must visit Tobago, which is the home of many more species that nest at several locations. These locations include St Giles Islands and Little Tobago, both of which are bird sanctuaries with restricted access. Seabirds may also be found close to shore at Store Bay, Buccoo, Mount Irvine and Plymouth on the west coast, and at Scarborough and Smith's Island on the east.

Other good birdwatching areas in Tobago include the Hillsborough Dam district, Grafton Estate, the Roxborough-Bloody Bay road and Charlotteville. Swamp and marshland in Tobago is limited, but some species can be found at Bon Accord and Friendship estates (which are private) and at Buccoo.

The above is by no means a complete list of the best sites for birdwatching, but it does provide some suggestions for the beginner. You will soon establish your own favourite spots.

Some useful references

A Guide to the Birds of Trinidad and Tobago. Richard ffrench. 1980, Harrowood Books, Pennsylvania.

Birds of the West Indies. James Bond. 1979, Collins, London.

A Guide to the Birds of Venezuela. R.M. de Schauensee and W.H. Phelps. 1978, Princeton University Press, New Jersey.

Birds of North America. C.S. Robbins, B. Bruun and H.S. Zim. 1983, Golden Press, New York.

Nature Trails of Trinidad. Richard ffrench and Peter Bacon. 1982, S.M. Publications, Port of Spain.

Living World The Journal of the Trinidad and Tobago Field Naturalists' Club. Published every two years.

Naturalist Magazine S.M. Publications, Port of Spain. Nine issues a year.

1
Gardens and parks

Palm Tanager (see page 11)

Blue-gray Tanager

White-lined Tanager, ♀

Blue-gray Tanager

Thraupis episcopus

Length: 17 cm (7 inches)

Family: Tanagers

One of the most popular on both islands, this species, known locally as 'Blue Jean', is found chiefly in cultivated areas and suburban districts, as well as in light woodlands and forest edges. Blue-gray Tanagers are often seen around houses and gardens, flying about in noisy and restless groups. Generally bluish-grey in colour, the upperparts are brighter blue and there is a vivid violet-blue patch on each wing-covert. The Tobagan birds are darker and more brilliantly coloured than their Trinidadian counterparts. The call-notes are a series of squeaky, high-pitched sounds without a regular pattern.

The Blue-gray Tanager feeds on fruits of many kinds, including tomatoes and other commercially-grown vegetables; it also takes insects, either from the air or from amidst foliage. Breeding is mainly between March and July and nests are usually high up in trees. The eggs are incubated for 14 days; the fledging period is 17 days.

Palm Tanager

Thraupis palmarum

Length: 17 cm (7 inches)

Family: Tanagers

This species is so closely related to the Blue-gray Tanager that some think that they may in fact be the same species. Like the Blue-gray, the Palm Tanager inhabits cultivated areas and suburban districts, but, true to its name, it seems to favour palms and generally feeds at a higher level above ground. Known locally as 'Palmiste', it is common on Trinidad and has been discovered recently on Tobago in various localities. Generally dull olive-green, it has yellowish wing-coverts and dark primaries, so in flight it appears to have a pale wing-bar (see page 9). Some individuals show distinctly bluish upperparts and are probably hybrids with the Blue-gray Tanager. The song is almost indistinguishable from that of the Blue-gray.

It feeds on fruit, nectar and insects by foraging among palms and other trees which have small berries, often hanging upside down from large palm-leaves. Nests are built in palms or under the eaves of houses. This is a restless bird which is full of 'nervous energy'.

White-lined Tanager

Tachyphonus rufus

Length: 18 cm (7½ inches)

Family: Tanagers

Sometimes called 'the Parson', this attractive and lively bird is common

11

on both islands in suburban districts as well as in cultivated areas and at the edge of forests. Superficially resembling a grackle, the male is glossy black all over, except for the under wing-coverts and a small patch on the upper coverts which are white (this is visible only when the bird is flying). In addition, the bill is shorter than the grackle's, and the lower mandible is whitish at the base. The female is entirely rufous brown. As the pair frequently associate together they may easily be identified. The song is a musical repeated phrase.

This species feeds largely on fruit and nectar, but insects are also eaten; it is attracted to over-ripe fruit on bird-tables. The nest is a large cup of leaves, usually situated in thick vegetation, sometimes in a garden shrub. The eggs are whitish and beautifully marked with dark brown.

Bananaquit   *Coereba flaveola*

Length: 10 cm (4 inches)   Family: Honeycreepers

Known locally as 'Sucrier' or 'Sugarbird', this species must be one of the most abundant to be found on both islands. It lives in almost every type of habitat: high mountains; rain forests; suburban and cultivated areas; even along the edges of mangrove swamps and sea-coasts. Its extreme abundance is partly due to its frequent breeding. It is a tiny bird which is variable in plumage. On our islands, the adult is black above with white superciliary streaks and wing-patches, and a yellow rump; below, it is mostly bright yellow. The short, black bill is slightly decurved. The song is a squeaky chatter.

Feeding principally on nectar, this bird may be readily attracted by sugar, syrup or over-ripe bananas, and as a result may become exceedingly tame. It builds a conspicuous nest: a sphere made of grass and leaves with a side entrance protected by a 'porch' above. Apart from the usual nest which is constructed for breeding, Bananaquits also build sleeping nests which are more roughly made. These nests are placed in a variety of sites, ranging from tree branches to artificial situations such as mailboxes.

Tropical Mockingbird   *Mimus gilvus*

Length: 25 cm (10 inches)   Family: Mockingbirds

A comparatively recent (early 20th century) arrival to Trinidad, this species is now widespread in suburban areas on both islands. It seems to be spreading into open country and even into clearings on the edge

Bananaquit

Tropical Mockingbird

Great Kiskadee

Barred Antshrike ♀

Copper-rumped Hummingbird

Black-throated Mango, ♀

of forests. It is less common in mountainous regions but is frequently found amidst the deciduous light forests of offshore islands. Unmistakable in appearance, it is grey above with dark eyestreaks, white superciliary streaks and whitish underparts; most conspicuous is the long, white-tipped tail. It is an indefatigable and attractive singer, especially in the early morning when it is one of the first birds to sing. In Tobago, the Tropical Mockingbird is known as 'Day Clean'.

An extremely aggressive species, it will not tolerate other birds of any species on its territory, and will chase and fight intruders until victorious. In gardens, owls, hawks, snakes, large lizards and even domestic animals may be attacked. The nest is a large, untidy cup of sticks, often placed in a low tree or bush. The three blue eggs are spotted with brown.

Great Kiskadee   *Pitangus sulphuratus*

Length: 22 cm (9 inches)   Family: Tyrant Flycatchers

This is probably the best-known bird in Trinidad, but it is not normally found in Tobago. It is widespread in suburban gardens and open country with scattered trees and may also be seen in mangrove swamps and on the edge of forests. The upperparts are dark brown as are the wings which are edged with rufous. The head is black (apart from a concealed yellow crest that is raised in moments of excitement) with a broad white streak around it. The underparts are bright yellow. The bill is heavy and strong. Though very similar to the Boat-billed Flycatcher (*Megarhynchus pitangua*) in appearance, Kiskadees may always be distinguished by their well-known cry, *Kis-ka-dee*.

This bird feeds on almost anything, but especially large insects and berries and it readily comes for scraps. The nest is a large untidy ball of grass with a side entrance and is usually situated in a tree or wedged against a telephone pole. The adults resolutely defend the area.

Barred Antshrike   *Thamnophilus doliatus*

Length: 15 cm (6 inches)   Family: Antbirds

This engaging, dumpy little bird is often seen in suburban gardens and light woodland on both islands, where its trusting nature frequently brings it into contact with humans. It is less commonly found in forest edges or at higher altitudes of up to 600 m (2000 feet). In most antbirds the sexes differ from each other in appearance, the males being predominantly black and the females brown. In this species the male is barred black and white all over; it has a noticeable crest and a short tail. The female is largely chestnut brown and is also crested. The call is a chuckling series, *ka-ka-ka*, accelerating towards the end. While calling, the bird wags its tail rapidly.

This antbird tends to skulk in low bushes, and its flight is short and rather weak. It feeds on small insects and is rarely seen high in trees. The nest is a flimsy hammock, suspended below a fork in a small plant, where both sexes incubate the eggs and care for the young. Two spotted eggs are laid.

Copper-rumped Hummingbird *Amazilia tobaci*

Length: 10 cm (4 inches)   Family: Hummingbirds

Of all the 16 members of this family that are known in our islands, this is the most commonly seen on both islands. It is found in a variety of habitats, from gardens and open country to cultivated land and the edge of forests, even up to 600 m (2000 feet). The sexes are similar in appearance: mainly brilliant iridescent green above and below, with coppery bronze on the lower back and tiny white tufts at the thighs; the bill is fairly short and straight. Apart from a twittering call and a single *tsip*, given while feeding, this species has a recognisable song, a series of three or four high-pitched notes, e.g. *tee-tee-tyu*.

Being very aggressive in defence of its territory, this hummingbird will attack any other bird, especially early in the year during its breeding season. Its nest is a small cup of plant-down which is usually placed on a small branch, but sometimes it is attached to wires or to another unlikely object. Incubation and fledging last for five weeks or more.

Black-throated Mango *Anthracothorax nigricollis*

Length: 11 cm (4½ inches)   Family: Hummingbirds

This bird is wide-ranging on both islands. It can be seen in gardens, in open country with scattered trees and in the edges of forest, from sea-level to mountain ridges. It seems to be largely absent from September to December, possibly because it migrates to the continent. One of the larger hummers, this species is bronze-green above with a purple tail. Males are black below with iridescent blue bordering the throat; females are white below with a prominent black stripe from chin to abdomen. The fairly long bill is slightly decurved.

It feeds on small insects, which are often caught in flight, and on the nectar of a wide variety of plants. The nest is a cup built of plant down and decorated with lichen. It is placed in an open position on a thin branch, usually quite high in a tree. Males display by spreading their colourful tails wide as they perch, so that the light shines through the feathers.

Ferruginous Pygmy-owl
Glaucidium brasilianum

Length: 15 cm (6 inches)   Family: Owls

Known locally as 'Jumbie Bird', and associated with superstition, this tiny owl is the most commonly encountered member of its family. This is partly because it is often about during the day as well as at night. It is the only small owl without ear-tufts, and is generally brown with white streaks and spots. Unknown in Tobago but common in Trinidad, it is found in forests and semi-open country with scattered trees, including suburban areas. The call is a long series of even-toned hoots, varied sometimes by a musical 'chirruping' note.

Like most owls, the Pygmy-owl nests in tree-hollows. It feeds on small creatures such as lizards and insects. Although it has rarely been recorded eating birds, its presence always provokes violent reactions from numbers of small birds, which gather round to mob and chase

Ferruginous Pygmy-owl

Smooth-billed Ani

the little owl. Imitation of its call will thus attract a number of small birds.

Smooth-billed Ani

Crotophaga ani

Length: 30 cm (12 inches)

Family: Cuckoos

Also called 'Merle Corbeau', this bird inhabits open country, gardens, parks and urban areas in both islands. Black all over, it is distinguished by its strange, parrot-shaped beak, its short, rounded wings and its long tail, which it raises to balance itself on landing. Its commonest call is a whining, two-tone *oo-leek*.

Anis, like other cuckoos, live mostly on grasshoppers and other insects. They are highly gregarious, feeding and living together in flocks of about 12 birds; they even nest in one large communal nest, where the females in the group may deposit up to 29 chalky-white eggs. Several birds may incubate together, and the young are fed and guarded by all the adults in the group. A larger species, the Greater Ani, *Crotophaga major*, inhabits mainly marshy areas.

18

White-tipped Dove

White-tipped Dove
Leptotila verreauxi

Length: 27 cm (11 inches)   Family: Pigeons and Doves

Generally known as 'Mountain Dove', this species is in fact much more common in secondary scrub and suburban districts than in mountainous areas. It is the only species of its size and colouring in Tobago, but in Trinidad it might well be confused with a similar species, the Grey-fronted Dove (*L. rufaxilla*), which does inhabit mountain forests. The White-tipped is greyish-brown above and white below, with a broad white tip to the tail. A close-up view will disclose that the bare eye-ring is *blue* (whereas it is *red* in the Grey-fronted).

Rarely flying high, this dove walks on the ground or flies among low trees and bushes. It is usually found alone or with a mate, rather than in a group. The nest is made of twigs or grass and is placed in the fork of a small tree, often quite low down. As with all members of this family, white eggs are laid.

Carib Grackle
Quiscalus lugubris

Length: 26 cm (10½ inches)   Family: Orioles and Blackbirds

Generally known as 'Blackbird' or, sometimes, 'Boat-tail', this species is smaller than similar members of the family that are found in North America and the Greater Antilles. The male is a glossy purplish-black with a long, keel-shaped tail; his bill is quite long and decurved, and his eyes are white. The female is similar but smaller and with a more regular tail. The immature is brownish-black with brown eyes. Call-notes are remarkable, being a series of harsh clucks and squeaks, often ending with a ringing bell-like note. Although the species is known throughout the Lesser Antilles, its dialect from Grenada and Barbados northwards can readily be distinguished from that of our islands.

Common in urban and suburban areas, the grackle sometimes feeds on grain and other seeds on open savannahs and rice-fields; it also takes many harmful insects. It readily comes to feeding tables for scraps. A gregarious species, it nests in small groups and roosts in massive numbers, notably amongst the Caroni mangroves.

Yellow Oriole
Icterus nigrogularis

Length: 20 cm (8 inches)   Family: Orioles and Blackbirds

By far the most common of the three oriole species that occur on Trinidad, this species, also known as the Small Cornbird, is widespread in suburban areas, in open woodland and along the edges of mangrove swamps. Generally bright yellow with black lores, tail and throat, the adult sometimes has a golden head (thus its other name, Golden Oriole). The wings are black with white edges. Immature birds are dull yellow and lack most of the black features. The call varies from a harsh, repeated *cack* to a musical, flute-like phrase of three to five notes.

It feeds largely on insects and other invertebrates, taken from amongst foliage, but also eats berries, small fruits, and nectar from a variety of flowering shrubs and trees. The nest is a pendulous tube of grass or palm fibres, and is about 45 cm (18 inches) long with the entrance hole near the top. It is slung from a branch of medium height. Sometimes the Piratic Flycatcher forces the parents to abandon their nest; they usually build another close by.

Carib Grackle

Yellow Oriole

Saffron Finch

Saffron Finch
Sicalis flaveola

Length: 14 cm (5½ inches)   Family: Finches and Seedeaters

This canary-like bird is common in Trinidad. It is found on savannahs or semi-open country with large trees, especially on housing estates where close-cut lawns are abundant. The adult is bright yellow with an orange crown. It is more thickset and has a shorter, thicker beak than the otherwise similar Yellow Warbler. Immatures are generally grey, often with a pale yellow breast-band. The call is an incisive *chink*, and the song a musical phrase of several repeated notes.

The Saffron Finch feeds largely on grass-seeds but also eats seeds of other plants. The nest is rarely built by the parents who prefer to use abandoned Oriole nests, to the inside of which they may add further material. However, occasionally they construct a cup nest in a tree-hollow or in one of a variety of artificial sites. Outside the breeding-season (which is centred around August) many of these finches, especially the immatures, form loose flocks and feed in groups.

2
Open country and scrubland

Silver-beaked Tanager, ♂ *(see page 34)*

Fork-tailed Flycatcher

Tyrannus savana

Length: 40 cm (16 inches)　　　　　Family: Tyrant Flycatchers

Most commonly found on savannahs and in open country, this species, locally called 'Scissors-tail', does occasionally visit the foothills of the Northern Range. Two distinct populations are known on our islands: the common one migrates from Argentina and Chile, wintering in northern South America between May and October; the less common race, distinguished by its paler back, is seen between November and February. Neither have yet been found to breed locally. With grey upperparts, a black head and white underparts, this spectacular flycatcher is best distinguished by its extremely long outer tail feathers (28 cm (11 inches) in the male; 18 cm (7 inches) in the female). However, many birds moult these feathers between June and September, so are seen without them.

This is a very gregarious bird, especially at the roost (which is often in mangroves). The birds fly to the roost in vast, loose flocks from the surrounding district during the last hour of daylight. In this flight the birds spread out and travel at about 30 m (100 feet) from the ground.

Fork-tailed Flycatcher

Tropical Kingbird

Tyrannus melancholicus

Length: 21 cm (8½ inches)   Family: Tyrant Flycatchers

Frequently mistaken for a Kiskadee, this species lives in open country. However, it is often seen perching on the tops of bare trees and electrical or telephone wires. It is duller in plumage than a Kiskadee, having a grey head with a dark eye-streak, grey to brown upper-parts, and a pale throat and breast; the rest of the underparts are paler yellow than a Kiskadee's. The call is a high-pitched twittering.

It feeds like a typical flycatcher, swooping out suddenly from a high perch to seize an insect in flight, and then returning to the original perch. Fearless in defence of its nest — an open cup of sticks placed high in a tree — the Kingbird attacks any other birds, including vultures and large hawks, that invade its territory. It is usually seen in pairs or alone.

Southern Lapwing

Vanellus chilensis

Length: 32 cm (13 inches)   Family: Plovers

Although rare before 1970, this species has been steadily increasing in numbers. It has spread throughout Trinidad to areas of rough, muddy

Tropical Kingbird

Southern Lapwing

Green-rumped Parrotlet

pasture with cattle, and is particularly common in Waller Field. It is rare in Tobago. Known throughout South America, it is common on the llanos. The Lapwing is a strikingly marked species with a crested head, black breast and black flight feathers with contrasting white coverts. Its call too is distinctive: a high-pitched series of repeated notes, heard at night as well as by day.

Breeding is now well established in Trinidad. The nest is merely a depression in the ground. As with all plovers, the young move away soon after hatching, their cryptic colouration making them hard to see on the ground. The food of this species comprises insects and other small arthropods.

Green-rumped Parrotlet

Forpus passerinus

Length: 13 cm (5 inches)   Family: Parrots

One of the smallest species in the parrot family, the Parrakeet (as it is generally called) is now widespread in lowland areas of Trinidad, although it was not recorded before the 20th century. It is less common in Tobago, where it may be an introduced species. A popular cage-bird, this tiny parrot is bright green all over (with a brilliant blue wing patch in males) and has a pale pink bill. The call is a squeaky chatter and is usually heard in chorus.

This species is very gregarious and the birds are almost always seen in groups of 10−20. At night they congregate to roost in large numbers. The Parrakeet flies with long, undulating swoops, calling frequently. It feeds on seeds and can cause damage to garden plants. It nests in a hole, exploiting not only natural cavities but also man-made structures, such as pipes and roof-eaves.

Ruddy Ground-dove

Columbina talpacoti

Length: 17 cm (7 inches)   Family: Pigeons and Doves

In both islands, this must be one of the commonest and most successful species to inhabit open areas. It is found in suburban districts, waste land and, especially, in newly cleared forest land. The second largest of four ground-dove species, it is characterised by its short legs and generally reddish-brown colouring. The male has a pale grey head and the female is a duller brown. In flight the black under-wing coverts are noticeable. The call is a soft rhythmical cooing, in which the first of two syllables is hardly audible.

It feeds on seeds and is frequently seen walking on the ground in pairs. It breeds several times a year, building flimsy nests of grass or small twigs that appear to be vulnerable to predation or natural disaster. Rival males fight with their wings, and 'nervous' wing-twitching is often seen in this species.

Striped Cuckoo
Tapera naevia

Length: 25 cm (10 inches)
Family: Cuckoos

This bird, with the strange local name of 'Wife-sick', is known more for its prominent call than for its appearance. Generally brown streaked with black above and paler below, it has a conspicuous white super-ciliary streak and a long tail. The usual call is a loud musical whistle of two notes, the second note being one semitone above the first; this call is repeated at intervals of 5–10 seconds and is made at night as well as by day. The Striped Cuckoo usually inhabits low-lying open country with scattered trees, but is also found in clearings which border forests.

This is the only one of the nine cuckoo species in Trinidad that is known to be parasitic. Its eggs are always laid in nests of one of the three spinetail species which are much smaller birds. Very little is known about how the cuckoo deposits its eggs. Its food consists of insects and spiders.

Ruby-topaz Hummingbird
Chrysolampis mosquitus

Length: 9 cm (3½ inches)
Family: Hummingbirds

This species is common in open country and gardens on both islands, especially between January and July (it probably migrates to the continent during the rest of the year). One of the most beautiful of our hummingbirds, the male is dark reddish-brown with a green gloss; his crown and nape are brilliant iridescent red and his throat and breast are iridescent gold (the iridescent colours show only when the light catches them at the correct angle). Females and immatures are duller than males. They are brownish above and grey below with a short black stripe from chin to breast, and a white tip on the outer tail. The bill is short and straight.

This hummingbird feeds on nectar taken from trees, such as samaan or fiddlewood, and from shrubs and small bushes. The nest is a tiny cup of plant-down and is built in the fork of a small branch which is often quite low in a tree.

28

Ruddy Ground-dove

Striped Cuckoo

Ruby-topaz Hummingbird, ♀

Red-breasted Blackbird, ♂

Red-breasted Blackbird   *Leistes militaris*

Length: 17 cm (7 inches)   Family: Orioles and Blackbirds

This is one of the most spectacular local birds. The male is sometimes known as the Soldier Bird because of his brilliant scarlet throat and underparts. The rest of the male's plumage is blackish-brown. The female's appearance is duller and paler but she has a prominent crown and eye-streaks, and a tinge of red about the breast. In Trinidad, the species is seen only in savannahs and drier marshlands. It has been recorded recently in western Tobago. The male's call is a short *chip*, followed by a long wheezing note, and is usually given during a display flight.

The Red-breasted Blackbird feeds largely on small invertebrates and seeds which are taken on the ground. The male often perches on a post or other prominent object. From here he flies at a steep incline for about 8 m (25 feet) in a display flight, returning with folded wings and showing off his brilliant plumage. The female builds a nest, a deep cup of grass, amidst long grass on the ground. However, although well-hidden, it does not often escape the notice of the parasitic Shiny Cowbird.

Shiny Cowbird, ♂

Shiny Cowbird

Molothrus bonariensis

Length: 18 cm (7½ inches)   Family: Orioles and Blackbirds

Possibly a recent immigrant into the West Indies from South America, this species is a common resident of open country, including urban and suburban areas. The male is a brilliant bluish-black, glossed with purple. Though resembling the Grackle and the White-lined Tanager, he can be distinguished by his brown eyes, shorter tail (often upturned) and short, dark bill. The female is dull brown, and the immature is distinguished by a yellowish superciliary streak. The male's song is a beautiful series of loud, musical whistles, mixed with 'bubbling' notes.

The diet of the Shiny Cowbird is similar to that of the Grackle, with which it frequently associates at the roost. The local name, 'Lazy Bird', stems from its parasitic (and cuckoo-like) habit of laying eggs in other birds' nests. Up to 20 species in Trinidad and Tobago are known to act as hosts to young cowbirds. The hosts' young are usually unable to compete with the fast-growing cowbirds. Cowbird eggs are nearly spherical and they vary in size and colour. Several females may lay their eggs in the same nest.

Blue-black Grassquit, ♂

Blue-black Grassquit

Volatinia jacarina

Length: 10 cm (4 inches)   Family: Finches and Seedeaters

This species is abundant and well-known on both islands. It has a variety of local names, including 'Ci-ci Zeb' and 'Johnny Jump-up'. It inhabits savannahs and open areas, including the edges of mangroves, cane fields and suburban districts. It is almost always seen near the ground. The male's plumage is glossy black with a dark blue tinge and its beak is short and stubby. The female is dull brown and has pale brown underparts with blackish streaks. The call is a nasal wheeze, *jwee*.

A true grass bird, this species is usually seen feeding on grass-seeds and, occasionally, insects. It feeds singly or in pairs, in rough ground. The nest is a small cup of grass which is placed low in a bush or in a clump of grass. The male performs an interesting display. He makes a short, upward jump from a perch (often a post or other vantage point) during which he spreads his wings and tail and utters the character-istic wheezing call. He lands back on the perch and repeats the performance every few seconds.

Yellow Warbler

Yellow Warbler

Dendroica petechia

Length: 11 cm (4½ inches)   Family: Wood Warblers

Twenty-three species of this family have been recorded on our islands, most of them only in very small numbers. Only two species are resident, but three others, including the Yellow Warbler, are common winter visitors from North America. The Yellow Warbler is frequently found in suburban areas, open country, mangroves and marshland, between early September and late March. In appearance, it is a smart little bird. It is yellow all over with slightly darker back and wings; the underparts are a particularly bright yellow and, in the male, they are streaked with chestnut. The call is a light *chip*; in March some males begin to sing a short musical phrase.

Individuals feed alone, hunting for tiny invertebrates in both trees and low vegetation. These birds rarely stay still; they search un-ceasingly on the undersides of leaves, calling frequently. They almost never alight on the ground, a habit which helps to distinguish them from the somewhat similar Saffron Finch, which feeds on grass seeds.

33

Silver-beaked Tanager

Ramphocelus carbo

Length: 17 cm (7 inches)

Family: Tanagers

This species is common in Trinidad but not in Tobago. It frequents light woodland and semi-open areas with bushy thickets. It is found on the edges of forests and in cultivated areas but rarely moves into the higher branches of trees. The male (see page 23) is outstandingly beautiful: a deep, velvety black, tinged with crimson especially around the head and breast. The bill is unusual, the upper mandible being black and the lower one being bluish-silver and much enlarged. The female is a duller reddish-brown, and her bill is less enlarged. The call is a sharp metallic *chip*.

This Tanager feeds mostly on fruit and nectar, especially from small shrubs and bromeliads close to the ground. Beetles, caterpillars and butterflies are also eaten. This species nests during the first seven months of the year, building a deep cup of leaves which may be situated in a bush or amidst long grass. The eggs are bright blue with dark brown markings.

3
Cultivated land with large trees

Rufous-browed Peppershrike *(see page 37)*

Bare-eyed Thrush

Yellow-bellied Elaenia

Rufous-browed Peppershrike

Cyclarhis gujanensis

Length: 16 cm (6½ inches)

Family: Vireos

Far more commonly heard than seen, this species usually escapes our notice because it keeps to the thick foliage of trees and rarely moves close to the ground. The peppershrike flies rather weakly and only for short distances. It is common in Trinidad but not in Tobago. It usually inhabits light woodland and cultivated and suburban areas; less frequently, it is found in true forest. More robust than the other members of its family, it is green above with a grey head and broad reddish superciliary streaks, and largely yellow underparts (see page 35). The beak is powerful and hooked. The call is a very musical phrase of several notes in a set cadence, which is repeated every few seconds: although the tunes vary, the same one may be repeated unaltered as many as 200 times.

It feeds on insects and spiders which it finds amongst thick foliage. It breeds during the rainy season and the nest — which is rarely seen — is built high in a tree. The nest is a flimsy 'hammock' which is slung in the fork of a branch.

Bare-eyed Thrush

Turdus nudigenis

Length: 24 cm (9½ inches)

Family: Thrushes

This well-known bird, also called the Gold-eye Thrush or the Big-eye Grive, is widespread in both islands. It inhabits semi-open suburban areas with large trees, secondary forest and cultivated estates. It is less common at higher altitudes and not known at all in true rain forest. Mainly brown in colour, its lower underparts are pale grey and its throat is streaked brown. Its most conspicuous feature is a large, bare, golden-yellow eye-ring, which gives it a strange staring appearance. Like many thrushes, it sings musically, but with less variety and power than most other Trinidadian thrushes. A common alarm note is a cat-like *keer-lee*.

This species feeds on a variety of soft fruits, insects and worms, mostly taken from the ground, and it readily comes for scraps. It nests during the early rainy season, building a substantial nest of mud and plant materials, which is situated in the fork of a tree. Usually three eggs are laid; they are blue with dark brown spots.

Yellow-bellied Elaenia

Elaenia flavogaster

Length: 16 cm (6½ inches)

Family: Tyrant Flycatchers

This is one of the most common members of its family on both the islands. It is found in light woodland, suburban gardens and on the edges of forest. The rather dull appearance of its greyish-brown upper plumage is relieved by two white wing-bars and pale greyish-yellow underparts. Most prominent is its crest which is almost always seen raised. Sometimes known as 'Jay' or 'Cutterhead', the Elaenia's call is a wheezing, drawn-out *zheer*. At dawn, it often sings a longer phrase persistently.

Elaenias feed on small insects, which may be caught in flight or hunted amongst foliage. They also take berries. The nest is usually built fairly high in a tree, and is a shallow cup of rootlets, decorated with lichen and often lined with feathers. Two spotted eggs are laid and most of the parental duties are undertaken by the female.

Buff-throated Woodcreeper

Xiphorhynchus guttatus

Length: 25 cm (10 inches)

Family: Woodcreepers

Most people mistake these birds for woodpeckers, but in fact they can be distinguished by both their method of feeding and their morphology. This species is generally reddish-brown, streaked with buff above and below. The reddish tail is stiff and it acts as a prop when the bird climbs a tree (like a woodpecker). The long, decurved bill is used as a probe and not to bore holes. The very penetrating call is a series of loud notes, *kew-kew-kew* etc., which tend to die away and to drop in pitch. Woodcreepers are found in forest and light woodland, including cultivated areas.

Feeding on invertebrates, woodcreepers not only probe tree bark and soft rotten wood for their food, but also frequently follow army ants to feed on the insects which are disturbed by the ants. The nests are tree-holes, and natural holes or crevices are usually used; woodcreepers do not bore nest-holes like woodpeckers.

Golden-olive Woodpecker

Piculus rubiginosus

Length: 20 cm (8 inches)

Family: Woodpeckers

Of the six species of woodpecker (also called Carpenter Birds) which are found in Trinidad, three, including this one, are also found in

Buff-throated Woodcreeper   *Golden-olive Woodpecker,* ♂

Tobago. They are widespread in woodland and some prefer large dead trees. The smaller species are frequently seen amidst lower vegetation; they climb spirally up a trunk, reach the top, fly off to another tree and repeat the process.

This species is golden-olive above and finely barred dark and yellow below. It has a distinctively marked head: the nape and moustachial streak are red, the forehead is dark blue and the rest of the face is yellowish white. The single piercing call-note, *keek*, is often uttered.

Its food consists largely of beetle larvae, but it will also take berries and is suspected of damaging cocoa pods. It nests in tree-hollows, and both parents share nesting duties. 'Drumming' is short and less noticeable in this species than in others.

Blue-crowned Motmot   *Momotus momota*

Length: 45 cm (18 inches)   Family: Motmots

This extraordinary bird is called 'King of the Woods' locally. It is notable as the only species from our islands to have a racquet-tipped tail; the barbs close to the tips of the long central tail-feathers fall out soon after maturity. Its strikingly beautiful plumage consists of green upperparts, a black crown which is encircled with turquoise, reddish underparts and a blue tail. The strong bill is black. Motmots sometimes inhabit forest undergrowth where they lurk in the deep shadow. However, in Tobago they are often seen in cultivated areas, perched on wires and branches beside roadbanks. The call is a deep, muffled hoot.

Motmots feed on a variety of invertebrates, but they also take fruit, small reptiles or fledglings, and can be tamed to come for scraps. They nest in long tunnels which are dug into banks; white eggs are laid at the far end of these.

Rufous-tailed Jacamar   *Galbula ruficauda*

Length: 25 cm (10 inches)   Family: Jacamars

This brilliant and excitable bird superficially resembles a very large hummingbird, however, it is more closely related to the motmots. Found amidst cultivated areas or in light woodland, it likes to perch in the open or on the edge of a clearing, from where it flies out at

Blue-crowned Motmot   *Rufous-tailed Jacamar, ♂*

intervals to catch its insect prey. The upperparts are iridescent bronze-green and the underparts are mostly reddish. Males differ from females in that they have white, rather than buff, throats. Both tail and bill are long and slim. The call is a high-pitched, rising series of notes, *pee-pee-pee* etc.

The Jacamar catches large flying insects, such as butterflies and dragonflies, and strips their wings off before eating them at the perch. Like the motmots, they tunnel into soft banks to lay eggs, but their nest-holes are smaller.

Orange-winged Parrot
Amazona amazonica

Length: 32 cm (13 inches)
Family: Parrots

This is a very common species on both islands, and it occasionally reaches pest proportions. In Trinidad, it is frequently found in low-land areas, especially swampy forests, but it also inhabits parts of the Northern Range. In Tobago, it is confined to the lighter areas of forest and cultivated land. The only Amazon parrot properly recorded on the islands, it can be recognised by its size, and by its plumage which is green with orange in both the wings and the tail. The

Orange-winged Parrot   *Crested Oropendola*

forehead and lores are blue, and there is some yellow on the crown and cheeks. The call is an inimitable scream, often heard in chorus.

Feeding on fruits, seeds and flowers, this parrot can cause considerable damage to cocoa cultivations. It nests in holes, often in a palm tree. It is often kept as a pet, but it is not known as a great talker.

Crested Oropendola
Psarocolius decumanus

Length: male: 42 cm (17 inches)
female: 32 cm (13 inches)

Family: Orioles and blackbirds

This extraordinary species, commonly called 'Yellowtail' or 'Corn-bird', is widespread on both islands in forest edges and in cultivated areas with large trees. Generally black with a chestnut rump, it has a long tail which is mostly bright yellow, a long whitish bill and bright blue eyes. The thin crest is often not visible. The call is variable, but consists mostly of loud, hoarse, gurgling notes, intermingled with clucks and unmusical trills. It is often accompanied by wing-flapping, feather rustling and a noise like that of tearing paper.

Gregarious and polygamous, Yellowtails nest in colonies of up to 50. The metre-long, stocking-shaped nests are made of strips of vegetation which are woven together by the female and attached to the branches of a tall tree. Each colony has one dominant male and several subordinate males, all of whom share the females who look after the incubation and the care of the young. Though fairly omnivorous, and inveterate nest-robbers, Yellowtails feed frequently on corn, citrus and cocoa, and so are considered to be agricultural pests.

4
The forest

Rufous-breasted Hermit (see page 45)

Pale-vented Pigeon

Spectacled Owl

Oilbird

Rufous-breasted Hermit
Glaucis hirsuta

Length: 12 cm (5 inches)   Family: Hummingbirds

One of the larger members of its family, this hummingbird is common on both islands. It prefers the shaded undergrowth in forests and cultivated land and is often found along mountain stream-beds. Mainly brown in colour, it is most easily distinguished by its long, decurved bill, its yellow lower mandible, and the prominent white tips to its rufous tail feathers. It is difficult to distinguish the male from the female.

It feeds largely on nectar from a variety of forest plants, but also takes small spiders and insects. The nest is a flimsy hammock of rootlets. It is attached by spider's web to the underside of a fern or similar shaped leaf, often overhanging a bank or stream-bed.

Two other Hermit species are found in Trinidad. The males of these species form leks, low down amidst forest vegetation. They sing monotonously and perform certain stylised movements for long periods every day throughout most of the year.

Pale-vented Pigeon
Columba cayennensis

Length: 30 cm (12 inches)   Family: Pigeons and Doves

This large pigeon is the only one which is commonly seen over the Main Ridge forests of Tobago. In Trinidad, it is usually restricted to open woodland in low-lying areas. A closely related species, the Scaled Pigeon (*C. speciosa*), inhabits the hill forests of Trinidad. Both birds are known locally as 'Ramier'. The Pale-vented Pigeon is generally dull purple with grey underparts, lower back and tail; the eye-ring and legs are red. The call is a deep, rhythmical cooing.

Like other pigeons, this species flies rapidly and directly, often quite high above the forest trees. It feeds on small wild fruit, such as that of the Hog Plum. A nest of sticks is built high in a tree, and two white eggs are laid.

Spectacled Owl
Pulsatrix perspicillata

Length: 45 cm (18 inches)   Family: Owls

This is the largest of the local owls in Trinidad, but it is not seen in Tobago. The adult is conspicuously marked, being dark brown on the upperparts, head and breast-band, buff on the lower underparts and having a whitish superciliary stripe which extends below the eye to give the bird a bespectacled appearance. The call is either a very deep hoot or a series of soft, breathy hoots which are only heard from close at hand. The habitat includes forests and cultivated areas, both on the plains and in the mountains. This species is widespread but not common.

Being entirely nocturnal, this species is rarely seen by day except when it is surprised at its roost-site. It feeds on a variety of small creatures, from insects to birds and rodents, and has been known to bother poultry farmers.

Oilbird
Steatornis caripensis

Length: 45 cm (18 inches)
Family: Oilbirds

Locally called 'Guacharo' or 'Diablotin', this extraordinary bird is highly specialised in several ways. It spends the day in dark caves or gorges emerging at night to feed on fruit. Known locations in Trinidad include caves at the Nature Centre, Mount Aripo and the northern Oropouche river. All the habitats are remote and fairly inaccessible, being either in deep forest or on a rugged sea coast. The adult, with its wing-span of over one metre, is rich brown in colour. It has a large, hooked bill and a long tail and so resembles both owls and nightjars in appearance.

Flying and feeding in near or total darkness, Oilbirds emit a series of clicks and the echoes from these enable them to navigate by sonar. This is the only nocturnal fruit-eating bird. It lives on the fruits of forest palms and certain other trees, which are located by smell. It breeds in caves and nests on mounds which are built up of regurgitated remains of fruit. In the cold environment of the caves, eggs and young mature very slowly, so the breeding season is very long.

Rufous-vented Chachalaca
Ortalis ruficauda

Length: 55 cm (22 inches)
Family: Guans

More commonly known as 'Cocrico', this turkey-like bird was chosen as the national bird of Tobago and so it adorns the country's coat of arms. It does not exist naturally in Trinidad, but occasional attempts to introduce it have been made. In Tobago, it frequents hill forests and is widespread in the secondary growth adjoining cultivated land, where farmers claim it damages crops. Certainly its numbers have increased with the abandonment of many farms after the 1963 hurricane. Normally remaining in thick undergrowth, the Chachalaca keeps in

Rufous-vented Chachalaca

contact with other members of its group by an extremely loud and raucous call. This call sounds like and gave rise to its common name, 'Cocrico'.

This species feeds largely on berries, small fruits and the young shoots of a variety of plants. It is also fond of dust-bathing, in the manner of domestic poultry.

Violaceous Trogon   *Trogon violaceus*

Length: 21 cm (8½ inches)   Family: Trogons

This is the smallest of the three members of this little-known family. It is widespread in Trinidad but not found in Tobago. It may be seen in forests or cultivated land with plenty of large trees. The male has dark blue head, upperparts and breast, and golden-yellow lower underparts. The long square-ended tail is finely barred black and white. Females are similar in appearance, but are dark grey instead of blue. The call is a rapid series of hoots.

Violaceous Trogon, ♂

Channel-billed Toucan

Trogons feed on both insects and small fruits which are taken in flight, after a long swoop from a perch. Their nests are in holes which are usually excavated from termite nests. Here they bring up their families, often amidst the termite colony.

Channel-billed Toucan   *Ramphastos vitellinus*

Length: 50 cm (20 inches)   Family: Toucans

This is the sole member of this well-known family to be found in Trinidad. It is not found in Tobago. It is well distributed throughout forest lands, but is often not noticed because it keeps largely to tree tops and rarely descends to near the ground. Generally black in colour, the Toucan is bright red on the breast and above and below the tail. The throat and the sides of neck are white and bordered below with orange. At the base of the great bill is a light blue bare patch around the eye. The call is a high-pitched, repeated single note and sounds rather like a yelping dog.

The Toucan feeds mostly on wild fruit but is also known to steal nestlings from other birds, and to eat insects. It hops about dexterously among the upper branches, sometimes in small groups. It nests in a tree-hole, which is often an abandoned woodpecker's hole and is usually high in the tree.

White-bearded Manakin   *Manacus manacus*

Length: 11 cm (4½ inches)   Family: Manakins

The three members of this family which are seen on our islands — two in Trinidad and one in Tobago — are some of the most interesting local birds.

This species usually inhabits deep forests, chiefly in the Northern Range, but is also found in cultivated areas with thick undergrowth. The male is black on the crown, the upper back, the wings and the tail. He has a grey lower back and is otherwise white. The female is olive green all over and is inconspicuous. Both male and female have orange legs. In flight, the male's wings 'whirr' audibly. The call-note is a musical *chirrup*. During display, males make a variety of sounds with their wings, including loud snaps, buzzes and rattles, which sound like fire-crackers (hence one local name, 'Casse Noisette').

The White-bearded Manakin feeds largely on small berries. The nest is a flimsy cup which is placed low in a forest sapling or fern. The females undertake all the nesting duties. The males gather at leks (see

Introduction), where they spend their days displaying to each other, and to visiting females, by jumping rapidly from perch to perch beside a prepared 'court'. Each male clears a small patch of forest ground of all vegetation; this is his territory or 'court' which he defends. Up to 70 courts may be found at a lek.

Bearded Bellbird

Procnias averano

Length: 28 cm (11 inches)   Family: Cotingas

This rather bizarre species inhabits deep forests in Trinidad. It is often very difficult to see, owing to its habit of perching high up amidst thick vegetation. Occasionally, a male will call from a bare branch. The male is unmistakable, being white with a brown head and black wings, and having many black wattles, resembling pieces of string, hanging from its throat. Females and immatures are olive green above and yellowish streaked with green below. The strong bill is rather short and is hooked at the tip. Males call an extremely loud *bock*, resembling the striking of an anvil, or a regular series of more musical notes, sounding a little like a bell (hence the local name, 'Campanero').

White-bearded Manakin, ♂   *Bearded Bellbird,* ♀

Bellbirds feed on highly nutritious fruit and resemble manakins in their breeding habits. Females attend the nest, while adult males gather in small groups at a lek, which is situated on specially chosen branches which are usually high on a forest tree. The males call and jump between branches, displaying their plumage.

Rufous-breasted Wren   *Thryothorus rutilus*

Length: 12 cm (5 inches)   Family: Wrens

Though less well-known than the House Wren (*Troglodytes aedon*), this engaging little bird is probably just as common. It inhabits light woodland, undergrowth and dense thickets in secondary forests. It rarely ventures out into the open, but skulks in low bushes. However, it is not particularly wary of humans. It is greyish-brown above, with a barred tail and a conspicuously speckled black and white throat. The breast is reddish and the lower underparts are brown. The birds frequently associate in pairs, calling to each other amidst the undergrowth in a 'duet' of alternating similar phrases; these are loud musical whistles, usually ending in a flourish.

It feeds on small insects which are taken from the ground or from

Rufous-breasted Wren

vegetation. The nest is a fairly large ball of leaves or grass with a wide side-entrance, and is usually situated amidst a tangle of low vegetation. Both parents attend to the young.

Both the Rufous-breasted and the House Wren are heavily parasitised by the Shiny Cowbird.

Bay-headed Tanager
Tangara gyrola

Length: 14 cm (5½ inches)   Family: Tanagers

This is the most common of the three medium-sized forest tanagers known in Trinidad; none of these are seen in Tobago. It is found in forest or secondary growth at all altitudes, but is particularly common in the Northern Range. The male and female are similar in appearance: generally green with a reddish-brown head; in fresh plumage some individuals show a golden tinge on the back. Immature birds lack the red head. Like the other forest tanagers, the call is a single metallic note or a light twittering.

It feeds mainly on small fruits from a wide variety of forest trees, vines and epiphytes. It also forages in small groups for insects among the foliage at all levels. The nest is a neat cup made mostly of moss and set in the fork of a small tree; the clutch of two eggs are white with brown markings.

Violaceous Euphonia
Euphonia violacea

Length: 11 cm (4½ inches)   Family: Tanagers

Commonly known as 'Semp', this little tanager is well-known in Trinidad where it is frequently kept in captivity as a pet. It is abundant in forests and secondary growth, including cultivated land, provided there are some large trees. The male is a handsome bird, glossy blue-black above with a little white on wings and tail; the underparts and a small patch in front of the crown are bright golden-yellow. The female and immatures are olive-green above and yellowish-olive below. The call is extremely musical and varied, with many different notes and squeaks. It often mimics other bird species, especially thrushes.

The Semp feeds principally on small fruits and berries, especially those of mistletoes and other epiphytes. The nest is a sphere of leaves and moss and it has a side entrance; it is often situated on the ground at the top of a bank. The three or four eggs are white marked with red.

52

Bay-headed Tanager

Violaceous Euphonia, ♂

Green Honeycreeper, ♂

Green Honeycreeper

Chlorophanes spiza

Length: 14 cm (5½ inches)

Family: Honeycreepers

Members of this group of birds are almost all brightly coloured and small. They move quickly through the upper branches of forest trees in search of nectar and small fruit. This species is quite common in the Northern Range of Trinidad, where it is found mainly in the canopy of large forest trees. The male is a bright metallic green, tinged with blue, and has a black cap which contrasts sharply with his yellow beak. The female is similar, but she is a paler green and lacks the black cap. The call is an incisive *chip*, which is similar to the call of the Yellow Warbler.

This species prefers to eat small fruits, which are plucked whole, but occasionally it will feed on nectar or insects. Its nest, which is not often found, is a small cup of leaves and rootlets. The eggs are white with brown spots, like those of all the members of this family.

5
Swamps, marshes and reservoirs

Black-bellied Whistling-duck (see page 60)

Cormorant

White-necked Heron

Snowy Egret

Cattle Egret

Olivaceous Cormorant

Phalacrocorax olivaceus

Length: 65 cm (26 inches)

Family: Cormorants

Sometimes mistaken for a large, black duck, the cormorant has a long neck and a hooked bill which distinguish it from the duck family. Cormorants perch on trees, posts and other projections and have a more upright stance than ducks which is more reminiscent of penguins. This species is glossy black all over, but around June the adult acquires a white plume at the side of the head. The throat pouch is dull orange.

Cormorants are found along the west coast of Trinidad, in inland reservoirs and, occasionally, in swamps and marshes. They have never been recorded breeding locally; they leave the island in August to breed on the South American continent, probably in the Orinoco delta. Scattered individuals remain during the 'off' season, but the majority are absent till December. Large numbers congregate at roosts, as can be seen in Pointe-a-Pierre. They feed by day in the freshwater reservoirs or at sea. Cormorants eat fish which they pursue underwater with great dexterity.

White-necked Heron

Ardea cocoi

Length: 112 cm (45 inches)

Family: Herons

Known to some (erroneously) as the 'Crane', this very large heron visits Trinidad during the dry season, preferring to breed in Venezuela later in the year. It resembles other large species, both in appearance and in its slow, stately manner of flight. It is generally grey, but has a white head, neck and breast, white thighs, and a black crown and flanks. The long bill is mostly yellow.

This heron stands motionless for long periods of time. It feeds, at the edge of a reservoir or in a marsh, by suddenly striking out at fish and other aquatic creatures. Unlike many other herons, this species tends to be solitary. It is quite rare in Trinidad, and very rare in Tobago.

Snowy Egret

Egretta thula

Length: 57 cm (23 inches)

Family: Herons

This beautiful heron is found on both islands in swamps and marshland, and along the coast where it feeds in shallow water. Some of these birds migrate to our islands during the North American winter, whilst others breed locally. Since it is all white, this species can be distinguished from other similar heron species only by its black bill, yellow lores, and black legs with contrasting bright yellow toes. When they are in breeding plumage, the adults have beautiful, elongated plumes on the head and back. Many years ago, these feathers were much in demand for the plume trade (now, thankfully, out of fashion).

Like other herons, this egret feeds largely on fish and other aquatic creatures. However, instead of standing still and patiently waiting for their prey, Snowy Egrets dash about excitedly, in shallow water, chasing their victims. Their nests are built low in mangrove trees.

Cattle Egret
Bubulcus ibis

Length: 52 cm (21 inches)   Family: Herons

A comparative newcomer to the New World, the Cattle Egret arrived from Africa early in the twentieth century, and was first recorded in Trinidad in 1951. Since then the population has expanded rapidly, so that it is now the most numerous heron species on our islands. It is similar in appearance to the Snowy Egret, except in that it is smaller and has a yellow bill and legs. In the breeding season, some of its white feathers are tinged with a buff or orange hue, and the legs and bill become reddish.

Cattle Egrets feed mostly on grasshoppers and other insects found in pastureland. Since domestic animals which graze, such as cattle, disturb these insects as they move about, the egrets often wait beside them, seizing the insects when they move. Likewise, they often follow tractors. Cattle Egrets nest and roost in mangroves, and they congregate at traditional sites (e.g. Caroni and Oropouche) every evening; great flocks can be seen moving to these roost-sites between 5.00 p.m. and 6.30 p.m. daily.

Green-backed Heron
Butorides striatus

Length: 40 cm (16 inches)   Family: Herons

Formerly called the Striated or the Green Heron, and known locally as 'Chuck' or 'Gaulin', this small heron is widespread on both islands. It is usually found on the banks of rivers, streams or reservoirs, or in freshwater marshland. The upperparts and wings are slate-grey with a greenish tinge; the crown is black, but the rest of the head, the neck and the sides of the breast are grey or (in Tobago) reddish; the lower underparts are pale with darker streaks and spots. The orange or yellow legs are much shorter than those of the egrets. The call is a sudden, sharp *kyow*.

A more solitary species than any of the egrets, this heron spends much of its time stalking its prey close to the water's edge. When stalking, it often stretches its body horizontally to attract less attention, and it keeps this posture for long periods. A nest of sticks is built in low trees close to water.

Scarlet Ibis

Eudocimus ruber

Length: 57 cm (23 inches)

Family: Ibises and Spoonbills

Undoubtedly Trinidad's most famous bird, the ibis was adopted as the National Bird in 1962; since then it has received official protection. Its numbers fluctuate in Trinidad because it is occasionally forced to migrate for safety to Venezuela; at their peak, the numbers in Caroni Swamp may reach 12,000. It is quite rare in Tobago. The bright scarlet adult, with black wing-tips and long curved bill, is unforgettable, but the mainly grey immature is much less spectacular.

The ibis roosts (and occasionally nests) in mangroves. It feeds over mud-flats and in shallow swamp lagoons, probing the mud for small

Green-backed Heron

Scarlet Ibis

crabs, but also taking shrimps and small fish. It is a very gregarious species, feeding, flying, nesting and roosting in large flocks. Every evening, during the last hour of daylight, the flocks converge upon the roost-site in the Caroni Swamp, creating a magnificent spectacle as they do so. Smaller numbers may be found in the Oropouche Lagoon and in other mangrove swamps.

Black-bellied Whistling-duck   *Dendrocygna autumnalis*

Length: 52 cm (21 inches)   Family: Ducks

There are three species of whistling-duck, sometimes called 'Tree-Ducks', known on our islands; the Black-bellied (see page 55) is the largest and most common. Whistling-ducks can be distinguished from other ducks by their longer necks and legs, their slower flight, and their habit of perching on trees or posts. This species is also notable for its bright red bill and conspicuous white wing patch which contrasts with the black flight feathers. Its high-pitched whistling call gives rise to its local name, 'Wi-chi-chi'.

Blue-winged Teal, ♂

Whistling-ducks are some of the few members of this family that breed locally. They nest at the height of the rainy season in marshy areas or rice fields. Unfortunately, this coincides with the hunting season, so the adults are unable to rear their families in peace. However, the Wildfowl Trust at Pointe-a-Pierre has encouraged the recovery of the Black-bellied Whistling-duck population by breeding the birds in captivity for subsequent release.

Blue-winged Teal

Anas discors

Length: 37 cm (15 inches)

Family: Ducks

This beautiful little duck is by far the most common of those duck species that migrate from North America during their off-season. Birds which have been banded (tagged) and then recovered in Trinidad and Tobago have originated mostly from north-central USA; some have come from Canada and some from New England. Birds arrive here in about October, and have usually left by the end of April. The female is a nondescript mottled brown; the adult male can be distinguished by a white crescent beside the eye. Both sexes have a large, pale blue wing-patch, which is visible only in flight.

Teal are found in both freshwater marshes and brackish mangrove swamps, often skulking amidst thick vegetation, where they feed on water-weed. They sometimes congregate into flocks, which are most active at dawn, dusk and even at night.

Purple Gallinule   *Porphyrula martinica*

Length: 32 cm (13 inches)   Family: Rails

Often loosely referred to as 'Water-Hen', this marsh-dwelling species does indeed resemble a small domestic fowl. However, its brilliant dark blue plumage sets it apart from a number of other species that may be found among the lilies and water-hyacinths of the typical Trinidadian marsh. It also has long yellow legs and extremely long toes which enable it to walk effectively on the marsh plants which float on the surface of the water. Seldom flying, and then only for short distances, the gallinule walks amidst vegetation, searching for flowers, seeds and leaves of certain plants; occasionally it climbs into a low bush and, very rarely, it swims.

The gallinule utters a variety of clucks, squawks and fowl-like cackling, usually from thick cover. Its nest is built amidst reeds or in a low bush. Up to seven eggs are laid; soon after hatching, the tiny, downy young leave the nest to follow their parents.

Wattled Jacana   *Jacana jacana*

Length: 25 cm (10 inches)   Family: Jacanas

Sometimes called 'Spurwing' or 'Lily-trotter', this marsh-dwelling bird is widespread in suitable habitats in Trinidad, but it is rarely seen in Tobago. The Wattled Jacana prefers freshwater areas to brackish mangrove swamps; typically, it is found in small ponds with lilies covering the water and reed-beds around the edge. Mostly dark reddish-brown, it shows pale yellow wings when flying; the legs are quite long and the toes are enormous. Immature birds are whitish below with a prominent black streak through the eye. This is a noisy species which calls with a high-pitched, rattling cry.

The Wattled Jacana feeds on aquatic creatures and makes its nest on a floating platform of lily leaves. The eggs are brown, beautifully patterned with black lines. The young are incubated and cared for by the male parent, who is extremely solicitous when they are newly hatched.

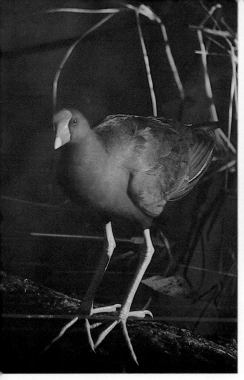

Purple Gallinule   *Wattled Jacana*

Lesser Golden Plover

Pluvialis dominica

Length: 25 cm (10 inches)   Family: Plovers

This is probably the most common of the nine plover species which have been recorded on our islands. Most of them are migrants from North America, where they breed on the arctic tundra. Some winter in the West Indies, others merely pass through on their way to Argentina or Chile. Usually, the adult has black underparts which are bordered by white; the upperparts are golden-brown, speckled with white. However, birds in winter plumage lack the black underparts, and many are seen in a transitional stage, with patches of black. The call is a high-pitched whistle.

Although occasionally it is seen on the coast, this species is usually found, from September to November, on flooded pastures, savannahs or golf-courses, forming loose flocks of up to 30 individuals. They have fairly long legs and comparatively short bills. Plovers are distinguishable from sandpipers by their common habit of running swiftly, stopping abruptly and then bending down to pick up food. Much time is spent standing motionless, often on one leg.

Lesser Golden Plover

Lesser Yellowlegs

Solitary Sandpiper

Lesser Yellowlegs

Tringa flavipes

Length: 25 cm (10 inches)

Family: Sandpipers

Twenty-five species from this family of shorebirds have been recorded on our islands. Most of them are seen regularly, either when they migrate from North to South America or when they spend the winter on the islands. With few exceptions, they leave to breed on the arctic tundra, but a few immature birds stay here over the summer months. The Lesser Yellowlegs is one of the larger and more striking members of this family, with its long, straight bill, and long, slender, bright yellow legs. Many of the species in this family are distinguishable from the others by only slight differences. One distinguishing point is the voice. This bird's call is a light but plaintive *kew* or *kew-kew*.

It spends most of its time in flooded savannahs or on the edges of muddy pools in marshes or swamps, and feeds on fish, molluscs, worms and small crustaceans. It tends to be quite gregarious, forming flocks of 15−30 birds, and often associates with its smaller cousins. It has a habit of bobbing its head and tilting its body when alarmed.

Solitary Sandpiper

Tringa solitaria

Length: 20 cm (8 inches)

Family: Sandpipers

The Solitary Sandpiper is fairly common on both islands. It is found in open areas, savannahs and marshes, and wherever streams and flooded ditches provide its preferred feeding conditions. It is rarely found on the coast but frequents freshwater areas. It is blackish-brown with faint spots and streaks above and white below; it has barred outer tail-feathers and a prominent, pale eye-ring. The bill and the legs are dark. The call is a fairly loud *peet* which is sometimes repeated, and is usually given when the bird is startled.

Unlike most other members of the family, this species does not form flocks. It is almost always found alone, feeding on invertebrates and small crustaceans along the edge of a pond or stream. When alarmed, it bobs its head sharply before flying away with a characteristically jerky motion. On landing, it often holds its wings open for a moment before settling. It is most common between August and March.

Semipalmated Sandpiper

Semipalmated Sandpiper

Calidris pusilla

Length: 15 cm (6 inches)   Family: Sandpipers

This sandpiper is nearly always found in flocks when migrating through or wintering on our islands. It is one of the smallest shorebird visitors and is known to North Americans as 'Peep'. Closely resembling several other small sandpipers, it can be distinguished by its greyish brown upperparts which are mottled and streaked with black, its white underparts, and its short black bill and black legs.

It breeds in arctic America and visits Trinidad and Tobago between August and April. However, a small number remain throughout the year.

Flocks of this sandpiper can comprise up to several thousand birds, which wheel and turn in flight with amazing unison and precision. The flock disperses to feed in shallow water or on mud-flats beside the sea. The birds peck at the surface of the mud for minute organisms. At rest, the flock is often tightly packed and extremely well camouflaged against the background of mud or rough, grassy banks.

Green Kingfisher, ♂

Green Kingfisher

Chlorocaryle americana

Length: 19 cm (7½ inches)

Family: Kingfishers

This is one of the two resident kingfishers; two migratory species may also be seen on the islands. All four species are found near water, especially in swamp-land, but also beside reservoirs and occasionally along the coast. The Green Kingfisher is the most common but, even so, it is very local in distribution. The male is dark bluish-green on the upperparts and head, and has white spots on the wings and tail; the breast is chestnut and the lower underparts white. The female is similar, but the underparts are buffy white and there are two green breast-bands. The dagger-shaped bill is long and powerful. Its call is an excited rattle.

Kingfishers feed on fish and aquatic insects, and they are usually seen flying rapidly and directly along a river, or perched on an overhanging branch. They nest in holes in the river-bank.

Yellow-throated Spinetail

Pied Water-tyrant

Yellow-throated Spinetail

Certhiaxis cinnamomea

Length: 15 cm (6 inches)

Family: Ovenbirds

Members of this obscure family vary greatly in their habits and habitat. They are all small brown birds which easily escape notice. This species is a common inhabitant of freshwater marshes. It is rich chestnut-brown above and white below, with a fairly long graduated tail. The call, which is often given, is a shrill rattle.

This spinetail feeds on small invertebrates which are found amidst low vegetation at the water's edge. It builds an enormous nest of twigs which is placed near the ground. The nest is shaped like an oblong vessel with a 'spout' through which the bird enters. Often the nest is decorated with pieces of snake-skin or other bright objects. All three spinetail species may be parasitised by the Striped Cuckoo. They are very tame near their nests and will even repair them in the presence of human beings.

Pied Water-tyrant

Fluvicola pica

Length: 15 cm (6 inches)

Family: Tyrant Flycatchers

This dapper little bird is common in Trinidad in freshwater marshland or muddy savannahs, in reservoirs and along the edges of mangrove swamps. It is found near the ground or amidst low bushes. The sexes are similar in appearance: white, with black wings, upper back and tail. The call is a conspicuous, nasal, buzzing note, *zhweeoo*, which is repeated at irregular intervals.

This flycatcher feeds on small insects which are found at the water's edge and are sometimes caught in flight. It flits about actively, constantly bobbing up and down and is rarely seen in repose. The nest is a ball of dried grass, mixed with feathers or wild cotton, with the opening at one side. It is quite conspicuous, being constructed on a stump or low branch, almost always over water, where most predators cannot reach it. Both parents attend the nest but, like other conspicuous nests, it is often visited by the Shiny Cowbird.

Yellow-hooded Blackbird

Agelaius icterocephalus

Length: 18 cm (7½ inches)

Family: Orioles and Blackbirds

The Yellow-hooded Blackbird is a resident of freshwater marshland in Trinidad, where it is abundant. It frequents the edges of mangrove

Yellow-hooded Blackbird ♂

swamps and is also found in rice fields, flooded savannahs and along the edges of cane fields. The male is most spectacular; it is glossy black with a brilliant yellow head, neck and upper breast, and black lores. The female is mainly brown with yellowish cheeks and throat. The call is a clucking note followed by a long drawn-out wheezing note.

This highly gregarious species feeds on a mixture of seeds, especially rice, and a variety of invertebrates. It takes grain crops but also destroys many insect pests. Breeding is communal and the nest, a deep cup of grass stems, is slung amidst reeds or other water plants, sometimes in low trees. Many nests, sometimes hundreds, are built together. The males are polygamous. The population is kept in check by heavy parasitism from the Shiny Cowbird.

6
The coast

Brown Pelican (see page 72)

Red-billed Tropicbird

Phaethon aethereus

Length: 100 cm (40 inches)

Family: Tropicbirds

The Red-billed Tropicbird is rarely seen off Trinidad. It is mainly confined to the islands of St. Giles and Little Tobago, where it nests between December and April. This beautiful seabird is mostly white, with some black on the wings, head and back. Its massive bill is bright red, and the two central tail feathers are elongated in the adult, extending for 50 cm (20 inches) and thus forming half its total length. Its call is a shrill scream which is sometimes repeated in a long series.

Tropicbirds feed at sea by plunging from a height into clear water and taking fish from near the surface. They do not flock but are found in small groups at the breeding grounds. One speckled egg is laid on the ground, often on a cliffside ledge or among rocks. While incubating or guarding the young, the parent is extremely tenacious, refusing to abandon the nest even when handled.

Magnificent Frigatebird

Fregata magnificens

Length: 100 cm (40 inches)

Family: Frigatebirds

Popularly known as the 'Man-o'-War Bird', the frigatebird is a familiar sight along the coasts of Trinidad and Tobago, gliding high above the sea or over the ridges of the Northern Range. In flight, it forms a distinctive silhouette, in the shape of a shallow W, its long wings spread to their two-metre (seven-foot) span. The long tail can occasionally be seen to be divided into a deep fork. The adult male is black all over, the female is black with a white breast, and the head and most of the underparts of the immature are white.

The frigatebird breeds on remote, undisturbed islands, such as St. Giles. It nests in low trees and lays one white egg. Both parents attend the nest, where the male often attracts his mate's attention by inflating his throat patch into a huge scarlet 'balloon'. The diet is usually fish, but frequently frigatebirds attack smaller seabirds, forcing them to disgorge their meals, which they then take.

Brown Pelican

Pelecanus occidentalis

Length: 120 cm (48 inches)

Family: Pelicans

This huge, heavy seabird, with its long bill and enormous pouch is well-known. The West Indian term 'Pillikin' refers not to this bird but

Red-billed Tropicbird   Magnificent Frigatebird, ♀

to the much smaller terns. Pelicans are known all along the coasts of both islands, and large flocks are sometimes found in the Gulf of Paria and near Plymouth. Generally brown, the adult has a white crown and a band of chestnut on the back of the head; the wings have a silvery pattern (see page 71).

Pelicans often swim in the sea or fly, often in formation, in flocks of about a dozen. When it spots fish, the pelican dives down at a steep incline, folding its wings just before hitting the water. As it emerges, with a pouch full of small fish, gulls and terns often crowd around to steal the food out of the pouch! Pelicans nest in trees, and are often disturbed by poachers.

Brown Booby   *Sula leucogaster*

Length: 75 cm (30 inches)   Family: Boobies

This seabird is common around the coasts of Tobago, but less common off Trinidad. Boobies keep further out to sea than gulls, terns and pelicans, flying low over the water and often gliding on their

Brown Booby

Laughing Gull

Brown Noddy

long, pointed wings. Adults are brown above and on the upper breast, and have white lower underparts; the stout, pointed beak is pale yellow. Immature birds are brown all over and their legs and beaks are duller than the adults'.

Although they usually hunt for food alone, boobies sometimes form loose flocks to exploit a rich food-supply. They feed on small fish, diving below the surface, often quite deep, to catch them. They breed on rocky islets off Tobago, making a simple nest of flattened grass or vegetation on the ground and usually on a cliff-side. One or two white eggs are laid, but it is rare for more than one chick to survive the long fledgling period.

Laughing Gull   *Larus atricilla*

Length: 40 cm (16 inches)   Family: Gulls and Terns

This is the only seagull that is common in our area. It is found on the coasts of both islands and breeds on small islands off the Tobago coast. Most of these birds leave the islands between November and March, but during the rest of the year they are extremely common in the main feeding areas in the Gulf of Paria, and near Scarborough or Plymouth, Tobago. During the breeding season, from April to August, adults develop a dark grey head; this becomes white in the 'off' season. The rest of the upperparts are grey, with black wing-tips, and the underparts are white. Gulls fly with a slower action than the rather similar terns.

The Laughing Gull feeds on fish and other marine organisms, which it takes from the surface of the sea or along the shore. The nest is merely a slight depression on the ground. The young gulls are largely brown.

Brown Noddy   *Anous stolidus*

Length: 37 cm (15 inches)   Family: Gulls and Terns

Many tern species are mostly white, but this tropical tern is distinguished by its dark brown plumage, with white forehead and wedge-shaped tail. It is widespread around Trinidad and Tobago and breeds on islands off Tobago and on Soldado Rock, mostly during the early months of the year. In the 'off' season they spend much time at sea, but many return at night to roost at their breeding grounds.

Noddies nest on cliff ledges or on rocky shores. The 'nest' is usually merely a hollow but occasionally it is built of sticks. The young chicks are either dark grey or whitish; the dark type predominates in our areas. The birds feed at the surface of the sea and are often attracted by shoals of small fish below, which cause them to gather in an excited flock to exploit the feast. Sometimes they settle on the water, like gulls.

Black Skimmer
Rynchops nigra

Length: 45 cm (18 inches) Family: Gulls and Terns

Although classified into this family, the Skimmer has a unique and extraordinary bill, the lower mandible being considerably larger than the upper. This species is mainly black above and white below; the base of the long bill is red, as are the short legs. Skimmers breed on mainland South America and visit Trinidad, especially the west and south coasts, mostly between May and November. Apart from the coasts, they also frequent marshes and reservoirs.

The Skimmer feeds by flying low over smooth water with the tip of the lower mandible skimming the surface. When it touches prey, the bill suddenly clamps shut. The birds often feed together in small flocks. They usually rest in flocks on mudbanks at the edge of the water.

Black Skimmer

7
The air

Peregrine Falcon (see page 82)

Black Vulture

Osprey

Black Vulture
Coragyps atratus

Length: 62 cm (25 inches)   Family: American Vultures

The 'Corbeau', as it is generally known, is probably the best known and least loved bird in Trinidad; oddly, it does not inhabit Tobago. It can be seen flying over all kinds of habitat and is particularly common at garbage dumps, along certain coasts and in other places where carrion is available. This species is more gregarious than the red-headed Turkey Vulture and it is often seen circling on thermal air-currents in large numbers. At night they congregate in roosts, usually in large trees. The Black Vulture is all black with pale bases to the primaries and can be distinguished from black hawks by its small head and, in flight, by its upturned wings.

This vulture locates its food by sight, whereas the Turkey Vulture uses its sense of smell. In addition to carrion, it feeds on coconuts. It makes no nest, and lays its eggs at the base of a large tree in light woodland.

Osprey
Pandion haliaetus

Length: 57 cm (23 inches)   Family: Hawks

Sometimes called the 'Fish Hawk', the Osprey visits our islands from its breeding grounds in North America. During the northern winter it is fairly common along the coast and over swamps and reservoirs; a few immature birds remain between May and September. The long wings, with their 1.8-metre (6-foot) span, bend noticeably, giving the bird a shallow W-shaped silhouette. The Osprey is mainly brown above and white below, and is one of the few hawks here with a white head; it has a prominent black streak through the eye. The call is a series of piercing, mewing notes.

After flying high above the water, the Osprey dives feet first to catch its prey, so causing a mighty splash. The prey is usually fish, which may be up to 45 cm (18 inches) long. Its talons are immensely strong and roughly serrated to enable it to grip fish securely.

Plumbeous Kite
Ictinia plumbea

Length: 35 cm (14 inches)   Family: Hawks

This beautiful bird is a typical kite in that it has a lighter build, longer tail and more pointed wings than other hawks. It is one of the smallest and most common of the eight species of kites found in

Trinidad. Although generally grey all over, it has reddish inner webs to the flight feathers so that in flight the spread wing shows some red. Its tail has narrow white bars and is square-ended. It has a musical, high-pitched call, *si-see-ooo*.

These kites arrive from the South American continent early in the year, nest high in trees in about May or June, and then leave again in about September. They feed on insects, which are caught in the air with the feet. The bird usually transfers its prey from foot to mouth while still in the air.

White Hawk
Leucopternis albicollis

Length: 45 cm (18 inches)
Family: Hawks

This beautiful bird of prey is a fairly common inhabitant of forested areas of Trinidad, especially those in the Northern Range. It is usually seen soaring high in the sky, where its pure white underparts, edged with black around the wing borders and at the base of the tail, clearly distinguish it from other hawks. The adult has a white head and neck, while the wings and some spots on the back are black; the upper tail is black with a white band. The call is a plaintive mewing note, *ker-wee*.

Feeding almost exclusively on reptiles, this species may sometimes be seen carrying snakes, including the deadly coral snake, in its talons. It hunts from a high perch where it looks out for its prey. The nest is built high in a forest tree and the single egg is bluish-white with brown markings.

Savannah Hawk
Heterospizias meridionalis

Length: 52 cm (21 inches)
Family: Hawks

This species is one which has benefited in recent years from the expansion of cattle ranching in the eastern and central districts of Trinidad; it was originally quite rare and localised, but may now be seen regularly at Waller Field and similar open savannah country. It is a large, long-legged hawk, generally reddish-brown in colour with black wing-tips and fine barring on the underparts. Its call is a loud scream which drops gradually in pitch.

Of all local hawks, this one seems to be the most adaptable; it will eat almost any small animal, including rodents, snakes, lizards, frogs, crabs, fish and insects. Its usual method of hunting is to sit on a high perch, watch for its prey, and drop suddenly down on to it. The nest is usually built high among the leaves of a large palm tree.

Plumbeous Kite   *White Hawk*

Savannah Hawk   *Swift*

Peregrine Falcon

Falco peregrinus

Length: 45 cm (18 inches)

Family: Falcons

Formerly called Duck Hawk, this magnificent falcon is renowned throughout the world for its speed, ferocity and aerial skill. Those found in our islands breed in the far north of America and migrate south in winter as far as Argentina and Chile. During the little time they spend here they are usually found along the coasts or in mangrove swamps where they hunt their prey. However, they may be seen flying over any habitat. The Peregrine has the typical long, pointed wings and slim tails of the falcons, but is larger than others in this family. Close up it shows a prominent black moustachial streak on the side of the head (see page 77).

The Peregrine Falcon feeds entirely on birds, usually small seabirds or marsh-dwelling sandpipers, which are taken in flight. Its normal method of hunting is to dive down onto its prey, overwhelming it by sheer speed, and then striking it with its powerful talons; the victim is killed by the impact.

Short-tailed Swift

Chaetura brachyura

Length: 10 cm (4 inches)

Family: Swifts

Superficially, swifts resemble swallows but they can be distinguished by their long, tapering wings, which appear curved in flight, and by their streamlined bodies. This species, which is one of five rather similar swifts, has wings which are much longer than its body. It is all black except for a pale brown area above and below the very short tail. It is best distinguished from the other swifts by its habitat: it is largely confined to low-lying districts, especially canefields and other open country, while the other swifts usually fly over forested hilly areas.

Swifts perch only when they are at the nest or roost; they spend the rest of the time flying rapidly about hunting for small insects, which they take in flight with their wide-open mouths. Their nests are small half-saucers of twigs, and are glued by the bird's saliva to a vertical surface which is usually in a hollow tree or a suitable man-made structure, such as a man-hole. Although rarely found in very large numbers, swifts tend to fly in loose flocks of 20–30 birds.

Gray-breasted Martin

Gray-breasted Martin

Progne chalybea

Length: 17 cm (7 inches)

Family: Swallows

Although some local dispersal takes place, this large swallow is resident on Trinidad (and its outlying islands) throughout the year. A similar species, the Caribbean Martin (*Progne dominicensis*), inhabits Tobago between February and October. Adults are glossy blue-black on the upperparts, with greyish brown breast and flanks and white lower underparts. The tail is forked but not markedly. It is distinguished from other swallows by its more robust appearance, and by its habit of flying high for much of the time. The call is a single twangy note.

These martins feed by catching small insects in flight. They often congregate on wires in large numbers, especially in the evening. They like to feed or bathe at reservoirs, flying down to take insects or water from the surface. Nests are built in holes or crevices which are often under house roofs and in cliff sides, but sometimes in pipes or on scaffolding. Both parents attend the nest.

Barn Swallow

Barn Swallow

Hirundo rustica

Length: 17 cm (7 inches)

Family: Swallows

This species is world-wide in distribution. It breeds in northern countries and migrates south for winter; our birds arrive as early as August and leave in April or May. During their stay here they are found over savannahs and open country, being especially common near cattle ranches where they exploit the rich food supply. Glossy dark blue on the upperparts, the adult has a chestnut forehead and throat, with paler chestnut lower underparts. This species is distinguished by its long outer tail feathers which form a deep fork. Like all swallows, these birds are light and graceful in flight. The call is an occasional light *chit*.

These swallows usually fly low over fields, and are especially common over rubbish tips or bagasse heaps, where small flying insects are taken. They often perch gregariously on wires or fences, but are soon away again to fly up and down over the plain.

Index

Ground-dove, ruddy, 27–8
Guacharo, 46, *44*
Gull, laughing, 75

Hawk: savannah, 80: white, 80
Hermit, rufous-breasted, 45, *43*
Heron: green-backed, 58–9; white-
  necked, 57
Heterospizias meridionalis, 80
Hirundo rustica, 84
Honeycreeper, green, 54
Hummingbird: copper-rumped, 16,
  14; ruby-topaz, 28

Ibis, scarlet, 59–60
Icterus nigrogularis, 20
Ictinia plumbea, 79–80

Jacamar, rufous-tailed, 40–1
Jacana, wattled, 62
Jacana jacana, 62
Jay, 38, *36*
Johnny Jump-up, 32
Jumbie bird, 17–18

King of the Woods, 39–40
Kingbird, tropical, 25
Kingfisher, green, 67
Kiskadee, Great, 13
Kite, plumbeous, 79–80

Lapwing, southern, 25–7
Larus atricilla, 75
Leistes militaris, 30
Leptotila: rufaxilla, 19; *verreauxi*, 19
Leucopternis albicollis, 80
Lily-trotter, 62

Manacus manacus, 49–50
Manakin, white-bearded, 49–50
Mango, black-throated, 16–17, *14*
Martin, gray-breasted, 83
Merle Corbeau, 18
Mimus gilvus, 12, 15, *13*
Mockingbird, Tropical, 12, 15, *13*
Molothrus bonariensis, 31
Momotus momota, 39–40

Motmot, blue-crowned, 39–40
Mountain Dove, 19

Noddy, brown, 75–6

Oilbird, 46, *44*
Oriole, yellow (golden), 20
Oropendola, crested, 42
Ortalis ruficauda, 46–7
Osprey, 79
Owl, spectacled, 45–6

Palmiste, 11, *9*
Pandion haliaetus, 79
Parrot, orange-winged, 41–2
Parrotlet, green-rumped, 27
Parson, 11–12
Pelecanus occidentalis, 72–3
Pelican, brown, 72–3
Peppershrike, rufous-browed, 37, *35*
Phaethon aethereus, 72
Phalacrocorax olivaceus, 57
Piculus rubiginosus, 38–9
Pigeon, pale-vented, 45
Pitangus sulphuratus, 15
Plover, lesser golden, 63
Pluvialis dominica, 63
Porphyrula martinica, 62
Procnias averano, 50–1
Progne chalybea, 83
Psarocolius decumanus, 42
Pulsatrix perspicillata, 45–6
Pygmy-owl, ferruginous, 17–18

Quiscalus lugubris, 20

Ramier, 45
Ramphastos vitellinus, 49
Ramphocelus carbo, 34, *23*
Rynchops nigra, 76

Sandpiper: semipalmated, 66:
  solitary, 65
Scissors-tail, 24
Semp, 52
Sicalis flaveola, 22
Skimmer, black, 76